In this WMG Writer's Guide, international bestselling author Kristine Kathryn Rusch helps writers navigate the changing tides of the publishing industry to make the best possible deal while retaining the rights to publish their works how and where they choose.

WMG Writer's Guide

Deal Breakers 2013
CONTRACT TERMS WRITERS SHOULD AVOID

KRISTINE KATHRYN RUSCH

WMG **PUBLISHING**

The WMG Writer's Guide Series

*Deal Breakers 2013:
Contract Terms Writers Should Avoid*

*The Pursuit of Perfection:
And How It Harms Writers*

*Surviving the Transition: How Writers Can Thrive
in the New World of Publishing*

*Think Like a Publisher: A Step-By-Step Guide
to Publishing Your Own Books*

Deal Breakers 2013

Copyright © 2013 Kristine Kathryn Rusch

All rights reserved

Published 2013 by WMG Publishing
www.wmgpublishing.com
Cover art © copyright Yudesign/Dreamstime
Book and cover design copyright © 2013 WMG Publishing
Cover design by Allyson Longueira/WMG Publishing
ISBN-13: 978-0-615-78957-6
ISBN-10: 0-615-78957-9

First published in slightly different form on www.kriswrites.com in the Business Rusch blog at the end of July to the middle of August, 2012. "Rights Reversion" was published in slightly different form in the Business Rusch blog in October, 2012. "Agents and Audits" was originally published as "Agents and Money" in slightly different form on the Business Rusch blog in November, 2012.

*This book is licensed for your personal enjoyment only.
All rights reserved. This book, or parts thereof, may not be reproduced in any form without permission.*

Contents

Introduction 1

Deal Breakers 5
Rights Reversion 31
Agents and Audits 41

About the Author 53

WMG Writer's Guide

Deal Breakers 2013
CONTRACT TERMS WRITERS SHOULD AVOID

Introduction

At some point, all writers will make a traditional publishing deal. Whether that deal is with a large traditional publishing company or with a small regional press, the writer will have to sign a contract. And the writer needs to understand that contract.

Writers are often desperate to get published. Or, in this modern age filled with easy self-publishing, writers want the "legitimacy" of an agent and a traditional book deal. Once writers have experience in traditional publishing and realize that it's not about legitimacy, but it's about business, those writers might choose to leave. Many of them, however, will do what I'm doing: they'll self-publish some things and publish others traditionally.

There's even a term for us now. We're called hybrid writers.

The bugaboo is the contract. The bugaboo is *always* the contract. Traditional publishing houses used to have relatively fair contracts. They don't any longer. If the writer handles a negotiation with a traditional publisher as if she's working with friends, she's making a very serious mistake.

In fact, any writer who lets her agent negotiate for her without having an intellectual properties attorney first vet the contract is also making a mistake. Traditional publishing contracts have gotten so complicated that agents (who have no legal training) can no longer handle the fine legal details with any degree of competency.

Traditional publishing houses have teams of attorneys developing their contracts. Writers need a team on their side to negotiate the contract.

The main reason is this: Traditional publishers have gone from wanting only the rights they need to demanding as many rights as they can get, not just for the book under consideration, but for all books the writer writes. If the writer wants to remain a hybrid writer—or even if she wants to leave and go to a different traditional publisher—then she must negotiate a good contract for herself.

I deal with that and much more in this short book. In 2011, the organization Novelists Inc. asked me to write about deal breakers in contracts. In 2012, they asked me for an update. I had to write an entirely new article, because contracts got so much worse in the interim.

I expect I will have to update this book every few years, as terms either get better or do as I fear and get much worse.

In this volume, you'll find the most important contract terms—or deal breakers—the ones that a writer should never allow in her contract. I deal only with book publishing here, not Hollywood contracts or contracts for comic books and games. I am not a lawyer, so what I'm giving you are guidelines for your negotiation, things to think about, and things to discuss with the attorney that you hire to help you negotiate.

I've also added two other sections. The first is on how to get your rights reverted to your traditionally published novel. The second is an important piece on auditing your agent. Both are things to consider.

Lastly, I have learned through the course of this series that writers are terrified to hire an attorney to handle their work. Writers believe that attorneys are both mean and expensive.

Most attorneys are friendly. Most give prospective clients a free consultation. Most charge by the hour, although many charge by the job. To review a simple contract will take an attorney who specializes in intellectual property at most two hours. Even at big city prices (hundreds per hour) that's much cheaper than hiring an agent at 15% of everything the book will earn. In the end, the attorney will probably cost $500 and the agent anywhere from $1,000 to $100,000 (or more) for work in which that agent has no expertise.

Most reputable attorneys also have payment plans. So if you can't afford $500 now, you might be able to afford $50 per month for 10 months. And many attorneys in the intellectual property field have set fees to look over standard American publishing contracts, standard foreign contracts, and so on. The fees mount up, as one attorney told me, when the client doesn't know what he wants.

So, this little guide should help you figure out what you want. It'll also help you figure out where your lines in the sand should be drawn. They're probably different than my lines. And that's just fine. We have different dreams and goals, after all.

I just want you to be aware of the pitfalls out there, and I hope I can help you avoid some of them. I want you to make the best deal possible *for you* so that your writing will grow and thrive.

Bad business practices and bad contracts destroy more writing careers than bad novels. Please make sure your business practices are as good as your prose.

Good luck!

—*Kristine Kathryn Rusch*
Lincoln City, Oregon
February 17, 2013

Deal Breakers

For the bulk of my thirty-year career in publishing, the industry has remained the same. In fact, the industry hadn't changed much since the end of the Second World War. Oh, there were changes—the rise of mass market paperbacks, the decline of the slick magazines, the introduction of computerized ordering—but those things happened slowly and usually one at a time.

In the past four years, the changes have come so quickly that it seems like we're on the Starship *Enterprise*, heading into a new galaxy at warp speed. You know that little wink of light when the starship goes into warp? That little dot was publishing in 2009. We've been at warp speed for four-plus years now and, unfortunately, our navigation systems don't work anymore (one word). We have no idea where we're going, but we're getting there fast.

A lot of writers are taking side trips, going into indie and/or self publishing. Even more of us have one foot in the indie world and the other in traditional publishing.

But the bulk of writers right now remain in traditional publishing, and *want to do so*. Writers don't want to trouble their pretty little heads thinking about business, so they expect their agents and their publishers to do that.

Unfortunately, the days when writers could farm out the business side of their writing are long gone. I've dealt with the changes a lot in my blog, which you can find at www.kristinekathrynrusch.com. I have also published a short book available titled *Surviving The Transition: How Writers Can Thrive In The New World of Publishing*. I suggest that you at least read some of this material, especially the blog post, "Writing Like It's 1999." It just might save your career.

Even though the changes in the publishing industry are moving at warp speed, traditional publishing itself still putters along at sublight. It still takes roughly two years from the sale of a new novel to the publication of that novel. And even those of us whose crystal balls have been polished recently have no real idea where the industry will be in two years.

Imagine, then, the difficulties of negotiating a contract that will remain in force for at least four or five years, when we're not even sure what we face two months from now. I negotiated a book deal two years ago that was great at the time, and that I would not sign today. I still have two books to deliver on that contract.

So even though this section is called "Deal Breakers," it should really be titled "Things To Consider While Negotiating Your Next Contract," a title which, let's be honest here, isn't nearly as sexy.

Before we get into the nitty-gritty, a few caveats. First, I am not a lawyer, and I do not play one on TV. I have not gone to law school, and I don't plan to. I have read thousands of publishing contracts—mine, those of my students, those of my colleagues, and those of the various publishing houses that used to employ me. So while I have some standing to write this section, I am not giving you legal advice. What follows is just my opinion. Got that?

Second, before you sell your next book to traditional publishers, go forth and read a book on negotiation. Yes, I know, the word "negotiation" isn't a pretty one. In fact, if your response to my last two sentences was either to cringe or to say blithely, "I have people for that," realize that I am talking to you in particular. You folks, with your head in the sand. Yeah, you. Stand up for a minute. I know negotiation scares you. It scares all of us. I'm not telling you to do the actual face-to-face stuff yourself. But I am telling you that you must guide these negotiations, either behind the scenes with your "people" or via e-mail or whatever cover of darkness you need to complete this messy job.

There are a lot of good books on negotiation, but I would be remiss if I didn't tell you about mine. It's a section of my *Freelancer's Survival Guide* called *How To Negotiate Anything*. You can read that section online for free on my blog or you can order the section as a stand-alone book (in trade or e-book), or as part of the gigantic *Freelancer's Guide* itself which has a trade paper edition as well as an e-book edition.

Here are the salient points from that section of the guide. (If you want explanation of any of those items, look at the books I recommended or the relevant chapters on my blog.)

First, the rules of negotiation:

1. Know What You Want.
2. Ask.
3. Be Prepared to Walk Away.
4. Stay Calm.
5. Never Reveal Your Entire Hand.
6. Don't Flip-Flop.

Second, the rules of contract negotiation:

1. Expect to Negotiate A Contract.
2. Imagine How the Terms of the Contract Will Impact You Over the Lifetime of the Contract.
3. Focus on What You Want.

4. Make Sure You Have An Equitable Way to Terminate The Contract.
5. Make Sure You Know How You'll Get Paid or How You Will Make Payments.
6. Control As Much of the Contract As Possible.
7. Once Both Parties Sign, Negotiation Is Over.

In the past, most writers did not think of any of these things, trusting their advisors to help them through the difficulties of negotiation. But with things in such flux, our advisors often have less information about the changes in publishing than we do. So we need to make decisions on our own.

A sidebar: I have always felt that writers should be actively involved in their careers. When I started teaching professional writers how to make breakthroughs in their careers, I wanted to put up a sign that said, *No Whining*. But that really doesn't work. Instead, my husband Dean Wesley Smith and I came up with a sign that reflects our philosophy:

You Are Responsible For Your Own Career.

You signed the contract. Your agent didn't sign it. You did. Your agent might have given you advice, but you took that advice. You took that deal, finalized that negotiation, worked with that company. If you got screwed, then it's your responsibility to make sure it never happens again. If you had incredible success, then congratulations. That success came from your actions as well.

Third, because things are changing so rapidly in this business, hire an intellectual properties attorney to help you negotiate your new contract. Yes, yes, I know. You have an agent, and you think that's what an agent's for. And, if this were the 20th century, you would be right.

But we are in a brave new world and agents have a serious handicap in modern negotiation: Most agents do *not* have law degrees. In the past, we could get away with having a non-lawyer do our negotiating for us. Publishing contracts fell into certain types, and it was pretty easy to know what contract terms meant. It was also easy to know what to ask for to improve those contract terms.

It is no longer easy, and it takes a legal mind to surf these rough waters. Your publisher has several lawyers on their team. You now need at least one lawyer on yours.

Okay. So, you have a team in place. You have an offer on the table. You know what you want.

Now let's talk about deal breakers. What is a deal breaker? It's the thing that you will not compromise on, not ever. Rather than compromise, you will walk away from the deal.

Trust me, your publisher has deal breakers. You need to know what yours are as well.

But I'm not going to talk in absolutes here, because each writer is different. We need different things, and we have different reasons for what we do.

Instead of being hard and firm and telling you to walk if these terms appear, let's discuss the places in a publishing contract where you should hold the line.

Those places are:

1. The Rights You Plan To License.
2. The Amount You Will Get Paid For That License.
3. The Number of Books You License in This Contract.
4. The Non-Compete Clause.
5. The Agent Clause.
6. Contract Termination.

Note that I'm using some terms unfamiliar to most of you. If you do not understand that you license copyright, get a copy of the most recent version of *The Copyright Handbook* from Nolo Press right now. You as a writer do not sell books; you license copyright. If that does not make sense to you, then you are at a serious disadvantage in *any* negotiation with anyone. You don't understand the basic tenet of your business. Buy this book immediately *and read it*.

I will explain the other terms in a minute, as I get to my six points.

1. The Rights You Plan To License.

The first thing every publishing contract states are the rights you will license to the publisher. In the past, I used to recommend that a writer only license North American Rights—that is, the right to sell the book in North America (in other words, the United States and Canada). Now, I recommend that you license World English Rights. Why the change, seemingly in the publisher's favor?

Here's why: Most writers stay in traditional publishing so that the publisher will do the work. It's hard to hold national boundary lines on e-books. In fact, in this modern world, it makes your fans angry. So rather than sell a North American edition only, let your publisher put the book up on Amazon Kindle and in all countries in the iBookstore. Gain English language readers all over the world.

But—and this is important—do *not* license World Rights. Keep the rights to your work in translation. Your publisher doesn't need to sell the translation rights for you. In this modern world, you can do that yourself. If your book is published in English worldwide, then other publishers will easily see it, and will want to translate it into their native language. Let them pay *you* for that, not your publisher.

In fact, hang onto as many rights as you can. Do not license movie rights or audio rights. I'd tell you not to license e-rights, but while that was possible in 2010, it's not possible any longer. Too many booksellers are going digital these days. No publisher is going to give up that market.

So in exchange for those e-rights, make sure you keep all the other rights in the work. License only *book* rights. Not enhanced e-rights, not application rights, not smart phone rights. Enhanced e-rights in particular are a place where publishers make outrageous rights grabs. Make sure you only license the rights to the *text* itself, not to text with pictures, text with audio. If you see something in the rights language that you do not understand, *do not agree to the terms or sign the contract* until you understand exactly what that language means.

Lately, I've had publishers here and in England (England especially) tell me that they don't need the rights they're buying. They're just adding those rights for "insurance" and they will "gift" those rights back to me if I but ask them. Look at the logic here. If they don't need the rights, then they shouldn't ask for them in the first place. This happens in particular with enhanced e-rights and new technology rights. That's where the biggest rights grabs are (at least as I write this in late 2012).

2. The Amount You Will Get Paid For That License.

This one's a tricky proposition. Because advances are going down significantly, while the demand for rights has gone up. Most established writers can make more money with self-publishing over the next two years than they can through their publisher.

The difference is that the publisher pays up front, and self-publishing does not.

There are a variety of ways to look at payment. The best way to examine what you're getting for the rights you license is the value you'll receive.

Note that I didn't say the money you will receive. Unless you're a *Times* bestseller, you're probably not going to be paid up front what you are worth, certainly not in these times.

So you need to examine the value of what the publisher offers. Here's how:

1. Do you need the up-front money to continue with your writing career? Can you live on that advance? If so, try to get the publisher to pay you on signing and acceptance of the finished manuscript. Limit your rewrites in your contract to no more than two.

2. Can your publisher get your book into markets that you cannot get your work into? (Make sure you know what's possible as well. See Dean Wesley Smith's short book *Think Like A Publisher* for that.) Are those markets worth going into? Two years ago, publishers could easily get your books into brick-and-mortar stores. Now, lots of brick-and-mortar stores are gone or cutting back on their titles. Is it worth losing a large chunk of your income for the opportunity to get into the reduced brick-and-mortar market?

3. Does your publisher do quality e-books? I can name several traditional publishers who do not do high quality e-books, trying to drive readers to hardcovers instead. If your publisher does a crappy e-book product and the market is moving to e-book, realize that your readers will blame you for the bad product, not your publisher.

4. Does your publisher do a timely e-book? Last year, one of my traditional publishers delayed the e-book of my latest release to the consternation of me and my fans. I lost hundreds of sales *weekly* because the publisher believed that the delay would increase sales of the trade paper. Even now, that particular publisher does not put my books in all e-book markets. So I constantly get letters from fans about inaccessibility of my books.

When my contract came up for renewal last year, I asked the publisher what he needed to satisfy the option. I also told him that unless he offered me a significant advance and a change in e-book policy, I would not license my book to his company. We parted ways quickly after that, and I can't be happier.

Why do I insist on an e-book that's published simultaneously with the hardcover? Because, in this madcap busy world, readers who want the book now will forget that the book exists when the e-edition finally appears six months from now. Each day a traditional publisher delays causes significant lost revenues—and subjects the writer to confused and angry e-mails.

5. Will your publisher promote your book? I don't necessarily mean whether or not your publisher will have an ad budget for your book. But is your publisher sending out galleys? Contacting the sales forces of local bookstores? Making sure the book bloggers know about the title? If your publisher isn't doing any of those things, then you're not getting value for your dollar.

Here's how I look at a book advance. If the publisher wants a lot of rights, the publisher must pay for them. With advances declining, it's less and less likely that a midlist writer can receive a good advance in exchange for the rights she's licensing.

Yet I continue to sell into traditional publishing. Why?

Because I'm using traditional publishing to advertise my indie-published titles under the same name. When *Wickedly Charming*, my Kristine Grayson novel, appeared from Sourcebooks, the sales of all of my indie-published Kristine Grayson novels jumped dramatically. They hit a higher plateau and have stayed on that plateau.

Sourcebooks is promoting Kristine Grayson in venues that I have yet to reach. Instead of me spending advertising dollars to get the word out on my book, I'm getting paid to advertise.

In the advertising business, they call what I'm doing a loss leader. I am losing some up-front money to bring someone to my product. Is it worthwhile? It was on the first Grayson book. Since I wrote this piece last year, I've published two more Grayson books with Sourcebooks. The increase in sales has not been as dramatic.

I suspect that the loss leader theory only works for a few books, rather than an entire series of them.

Which brings us to:

3. The Number of Books You License in This Contract

In the past, every writer wanted a multi-book contract. It gave us security, and it made sure that the publishing house put an effort into publishing our work. The publishing house had a lot of money and future profits at stake, so the house worked harder on multi-book contracts.

Now, with things changing as rapidly as they are, multi-book contracts no longer provide security. They might harm us by locking us into contract terms that won't be good for us in 2014 or 2015.

Right now, go with a one-book contract. It gives you flexibility to negotiate better terms for you in the future, terms we may not even be able to envision now. (Did you know what an app was in 2008? If you signed a multi-book contract that year, you are probably still fulfilling that contract. And it's out of date.)

4. The Non-Compete Clause

At the moment, traditional publishers, particularly the large companies (erroneously called The Big Six), are trying to control *everything* about a writer, from the rights she sells to the amount of money she makes. They also want what they're calling "a non-compete" clause.

In reality, it's a "do-not-do-business-without-our-permission" clause.

I did write about this in 2011, but I was a bit more lenient toward publishers than I am now. What changed? I certainly didn't. I believe that writers should protect their rights as much as possible.

What changed is this: publishers have started *requiring* non-compete clauses in almost all of their contracts, and are making those clauses a deal breaker *from the publisher's side*. In other words, the publisher will cancel the deal if you do not sign a non-compete. The choice you are given is this: either you let the publisher control your entire career just because you sold that publisher one book for $5000 or you walk.

If that's the choice you're given, *walk*. Hell, *run*.

You have other options now. You can go to a different traditional publisher if you want. You can publish that work yourself. *You're even better off putting that book in a drawer and not mailing to anyone than you are signing that clause.*

Got it?

Because the moment you sign that clause, you give over your entire career to a corporation that cares nothing for you. Even if the clause does not hold up in court (and quite honestly, I don't think the clause can hold up but again, I am not an attorney), you'd have to spend years not writing and litigating to prove me right.

What is the clause? Well, it's not an option clause. For almost twenty years, publishers have used the option clause to have dibs in an author's next book. In other words, the publisher got the right of first refusal on that book, and no one else could see it until the publisher made up his mind.

Properly negotiated, an option clause benefited the writer as well as the publisher, often by forcing the publisher to bid on the next book long before the first book came out. A bad option clause could prevent a writer from publishing another book for a year or two after the first book came out—and this was in the previous century.

But agents, attorneys, and most writers learned how to take the teeth out of an option clause. And those toothless option clauses remain, which is why I am not saying anything bad about an option clause. Your option clause will probably look fine.

You'll often find the non-compete clause in the same section of your contract as the option clause. The non-compete clause will look something like this:

The Author agrees that during the terms of this Agreement he will not, without the written permission of the Publisher, publish or authorize to be published any work under this name or any other, including blog posts, short stories, nonfiction articles, novels, or the like.

In other words, the contract will *prevent the writer from making a living* at his craft. I saw that clause in my first contract with Bantam Books fifteen years ago and hit the ceiling. (The word blog was not in it, of course.) I thought I was going to lose this rather large contract because no way in hell would I sign a document with that clause in it.

I demanded the clause's removal and got it with no fuss at all. Recently, however, writers have signed contracts with that clause because they were told the clause was a deal breaker. I know of at least two mystery writers who need their publisher's permission to put up a blog post. I know of several more who have had to get a document granting them blanket permission from their fiction publisher to write nonfiction.

Do you really want that to happen to you? Because it could if you sign this clause. Consider that the contract, like your mortgage, might get sold to another company you're entirely unfamiliar with at the moment. This recently happened to Avalon authors who had no idea when they signed their contracts that eventually Amazon would have the rights to publish those works. (I will deal with that in "Contract Termination" below.)

Your current publisher might not enforce that clause; the publisher/business your current publisher sells out to might enforce the clause, and make you pay damages for anything you've previously published after you signed the contract (and ignored the clause).

Worst case, right? Yes, it is. But before you sign a contract, you must imagine the worst-case scenario. The contract you negotiate should protect you from bad things, but you have to realize how bad those things can actually be.

Let's go back to the clause: It is ridiculous. It's there to prevent you from controlling your craft. According to that clause, your publisher is in charge of everything you write, *whether the publisher pays you for it or not*. Got that?

I have seen other versions of this clause, negotiated by (idiot) agents for their established clients. Those versions usually read something like this:

The Author agrees that, during the term of this Agreement, he will not, without the written permission of the Publisher, publish or authorize to be published any work substantially similar to the Work or which is likely to injure its sale or the merchandising of other rights herein.

This is only marginally better. Seriously. You're still asking your publisher's permission to write something. Granted, it's only under one name, and if your publisher withholds permission, you can start up a new pen name, but honestly…who signs this stuff? And what advisor thinks something like this is okay for a writer to sign?

Because the problem isn't with the publisher's permission. The problem here is two phrases: "substantially similar" and "likely to injure." Who decides if my funny fantasy novel about fairy-tale characters is substantially similar to my science fiction novels about the Moon? They are supposedly in the same genre—sf/f. Or what about my mystery series set in Chicago in the late 1960s? Is that substantially similar to the mysteries set on the Moon? They are both mysteries after all.

And who determines if those Moon mysteries "injure" the sales of the 1968 mysteries? Does the fact that I'm also publishing romance, a genre that many sf editors don't respect, "injure" the sales of my sf books?

See the problem?

It gets worse when you think about who gets to decide. Most writers will let their publishers decide. Those writers who challenge the publisher's decision will find their books, their careers, their livelihoods tied up in civil court, waiting for a judge to decide.

I have seen several versions of these clauses negotiated to death, with all kinds of phrases added in, but none of them are toothless, and all of them tie the writer's output to his publisher's permission.

For me, this clause is a deal breaker. No one controls my career but me. No one tells me what to write but me.

The best way to handle a non-compete clause is to refuse to sign one.

So…you take the non-compete clause out and you're in the clear, right?

Hell, no. Lately these publishers have been adding something in the boilerplate section of the contract (which most agents don't even read). A boilerplate section is the stuff that should remain the same from contract to contract—you negotiate it once, and it doesn't change. It's stock or formulaic language that covers expected things like insurance coverage and Acts of God. Some boilerplate can be changed and some can't.

In the boilerplate section is something called a warranty, and in it, you'll find language like:

The Author Warrants that the Work is original, and uses no material from any other source…

Things like that.

Only cagey publishers have started to add this:

The Author Warrants that she will not publish any other work until this contract is fully executed.

In other words, the Author can't publish anything until all the terms of the contract are met. Meaning that she cannot publish anything until the second or fifth or tenth book of the contract is published, and maybe, depending on the wording, not even then. She might not be able to publish until the book goes out of print.

If the book goes out of print.

Seriously, folks, watch out for this stuff. Take clauses like this out of the contract. If your publisher refuses to remove language like this from your contract *and you still sign it*, you will have no one to blame but yourself for your tanking writing career. Because you put your signature on a legal document giving someone else control of your output.

Let's look at the non-compete clause from yet another perspective—one of balance.

Technically, contracts should at least pretend to have balance between the parties. Theoretically, you and your publisher are equal partners in the venture of publishing a book, and your contract should reflect that. Contract law, from dozens of countries including ours, assumes that both parties are able to enter into the contract equally, with the same kind of knowledge and judgment.

If you can show, in court, that you've been swindled, bamboozled, or forced to sign a contract whose terms actively harm you, then the contract might—and I use the word "might" here on purpose—be canceled.

One of the things a judge will look at to see if one party is unfairly taken advantage of in the contract negotiation phase is balance. If the entire contract benefits only one party, then the contract is unbalanced, and argues—by its very existence—that the other party was taken advantage of.

The judge is not required to act here, and often will not. This is one of the many reasons I tell you to avoid court.

But let's explore balance for a moment:

If you are a professional writer *who makes her living on her writing*, and you have signed a contract that does not allow you to practice your trade, then there must be some similar consideration for the other party to make the contract balance.

In other words, if your publisher wants *you* to sign a non-compete clause, then your publisher should sign one as well.

If you ask for a non-compete as ridiculous as the one the publisher is asking of you, then it would read like this:

The Publisher agrees that during the terms of this Agreement he will not, without the written permission of the Author, publish or authorize to be published any work that might compete with the Work, including blog posts, short stories, nonfiction articles, novels, or the like.

Imagine a publisher signing that. Oh, you can't? Neither can I.

But let's dial it down a notch. Let's say you sell a vampire romance to Publisher A. If the contract has balance, then you can't publish a romance or a vampire book that might compete with yours—*and neither can your publisher*. Even if you limit the non-compete to two years, imagine telling your traditional publisher that they can't publish vampire books or romance books for two years after the publication of your novel.

Do you see *now* how wrong this clause is? You should not sign it because it's bad for you. If that argument doesn't sway you, then ask yourself if any reasonable business would sign a contract with a clause like that. Or if *any* business would sign a clause like that for *any* reason.

Your writing career is a business. Act like it.

Do not sign something that will stop you from practicing your trade.

Ever.

5. The Agent Clause

Agents have been abusing this clause for years now. *Agents*, not publishers, even though this clause is in a publishing contract between the writer and her publisher.

Once upon a time, publishers paid the writer directly and the writer paid the agent. Which is, frankly, how it should be. After all, the agent is someone *you* hired, not the publisher.

However, some brainy publisher got the idea that if Agent A has 20 clients with the publishing house, it's easier to write one check to Agent A than it is to write 20 checks to the writers. Agents liked this because that meant they didn't have to browbeat their writers to get the commission.

Paying the agent directly is not legal without the writer's permission. So some lawyer came up with the way to do this. It is the origin of the agent clause, which was, in reality, a payment clause. Checks sent to Agent A (at such-and-so address) counted as payment to Writer Z, and thus fulfilled the contract. *That's all.* If the writer signed the contract, then the clause became activated, and all payments went to Agent A.

The problem with this is, if you fire Agent A, you need an addendum to the contract, so that payment would go either directly to you or to Agent B, who is now your representative.

Well, that would screw Agent A out of money that you probably owed him. So the agent started adding words like "irrevocable" to the agent clause which, of course, he negotiated.

Then things went crazy. Agents started adding all kinds of things to the agent clause which are in the agent's interest, but no one else's. The agent would add things like "the agent represents the author on this book, and all foreign sales of this book" and so on.

Then the agents all seemed to come up with "agency coupled with an interest." The clause, which you find in most agent-negotiated publishing contracts, now says things like:

The Author hereby appoints Agent A irrevocably as the Agent in all matters pertaining to or arising from this Agreement...Such Agent is hereby fully empowered to act on behalf of the Author in all matters in any way arising out of this Agreement...All sums of money due to the Author under this Agreement shall be paid to and in the name of said Agent...The Author does also irrevocably assign and transfer to Agent A, as an agency coupled with an interest, and Agent A shall retain a sum equal to fifteen percent (15%) of all gross monies due and payable to the account of the Author under this Agreement."

Authors blithely sign this stuff. I refused, and cut things like "fully empowered" and "agency coupled with an interest" from my contracts. I authorized payment only. A few of my former agents balked; I fired them.

Why? First of all, I'm not assigning anyone anything "irrevocably"—certainly not someone I can fire for cause. *Especially* if my money goes through their account first. I will not "fully empower" anyone to act for me. (Some agents go so far as demanding legal power of attorney—which is something you should never give anyone. What that means is that they then have the right *to be you* in all legal matters. No. Do not give legal power of attorney to anyone without good cause—like you're dying and need someone to handle your accounts [and even then, it might not be a good idea].)

Finally let's discuss "agency coupled with an interest." What that means is this: *You are giving the agent ownership in your novel.* Ownership. They now have a 15% ownership of your book.

In theory. Technically, a two-party contract cannot hold one party to third-party terms. In other words, if you and Publisher K have a contract, it cannot bind you to do things for Agent A, because Agent A did not sign the contract.

Still, what's to stop Agent A from trying this? A lot of agents are doing it, and backing it up with a separate agent-writer contract, which I'll touch on in a moment. Absent the agent-writer contract, these clauses should not hold up in court.

In the past year, two examples held up my non-lawyerly reading of these clauses. First, the Ralph Vicinancza Agency tried to sue its writers under this clause. Ralph, who ran the business for decades, died suddenly, leaving his agency to heirs who had no idea how the publishing industry worked. However, they wanted their money, and they threatened to sue authors who wouldn't work with them.

A lot of negotiation happened, and a lot of behind-the-scenes maneuvering, which took nearly a year before everyone settled out of court. Writers lost entire books in time trying to hang onto their own income and reserve the right to hire an agent who actually knew what he was doing, instead of some relatives who had no idea what an agent was before their family member died.

That's but one example. The other, more important example, is an actual court case: *Peter Lampack Agency v. Grimes et.al.*

In 1996, Martha Grimes hired the Peter Lampack Agency (PLA) to represent her works. For those of you who don't know, she's a *New York Times* bestseller and a Grand Master in the mystery field.

In 2007, she fired PLA. At the time, she had a four-book contract with Penguin. That contract had an option on a book called *The Black Cat*. Grimes eventually sold *The Black Cat* to Penguin through another agent, and PLA sued, claiming—under the agency clause—that it had rights to any work deriving from that original contract.

Long story short, the case made it to New York court. The court decided that the agency clause only entitled PLA a 15% interest in the four-books named in the original contract, not in *The Black Cat*.

A victory, yes, but a minor one. Because Grimes fired PLA, and still has to deal with them to this day on books still in print.

Also, this victory—so far—only applies in the State of New York. It hasn't been tested elsewhere.

Finally, after this ruling, most major agencies required their writers to sign an agreement *with the agency* stating that the writer will follow all the terms of an agency clause in publishing contracts.

Some major agencies actually take 15% ownership in *everything* a writer writes, even if that writer never sells the product through the agency at all. This is becoming more and more common, and is worth an essay all its own.

The short version: never sign an agreement with your agent without letting your intellectual property attorney look over the agreement first and negotiate it for you.

Better yet, let your attorney negotiate all of your contracts and avoid the agent clause altogether. In fact, pay your agent out of your own pocket. Your money should never go to someone else first.

If you have an agent, pay them yourself. If they don't trust you to do so, then why should you trust them? If they get pissy, have an agency clause that *you* (or your attorney) writes, that splits payments—15% directly to the agent and 85% to you.

Of course, if you have an attorney negotiate your contracts, and you're dealing with the publisher yourself, why do you have an agent in the first place? Maybe it's time to get rid of this vestige of mid-20th century publishing and branch out on your own.

Finally, let's examine the sixth and final point:

6. Contract Termination

This is the part I had to revise the most heavily from last year. Publishers have gotten quite nasty about contracts. In short, they're refusing to let any contract terminate.

This is causing all kinds of problems for writers.

Last year, I suggested that writers needed to have a sunset clause in their contract. Contracts, by their very nature, need some sort of ending. They can't be "forever" or unlimited. They must have a limitation. For the past fifty years or so, the limitation in the U.S. publishing contracts has been what is called sales velocity. If the sales dip below a particular amount, then the writer can ask for a reversion.

In the past, sales were impossible if a book wasn't in a brick-and-mortar store. So if you couldn't find your book in a bookstore, and your friendly neighborhood bookseller couldn't order it, then the book was officially out of print. You would write a letter demanding your rights back, and your publisher would have six months to put the book back into print or the rights would revert to you. Simple (more or less), even if it was contingent on action by the writer (composing and mailing that letter).

The rise of print-on-demand and e-books changed the bookstore calculus. Now, a book could remain "in print" and "available" forever. With the click of a button, a publisher could send another copy of that book to the interested party.

So last year, I suggested this: *Define out of print this way: The book shall be deemed out of print if, after five years in print, the author is not receiving a royalty check of at least $500 per six-month period.*

In other words, your book has to have earned out its advance, and be paying you royalties of at least $1000 every single year.

Publishers are loathe to agree to this because it's not in their best interest. Negotiate on the number of years to recoup the advance—three years, five years, ten years—but never on the money. You have to be earning real money on this book for them to hang onto your rights indefinitely.

Shortly after I published this, a publisher friend of mine pointed out that such a small threshold is a tiny price for a publisher to pay to hold onto a book indefinitely. If the book doesn't earn $500 in real royalties in a time period, then the publisher could pay a $500 "bonus," to buy the right to remain in print.

I'm not sure that would work, but the point is a good one: any threshold that is based on sales or velocity or money can be worked around in the modern market.

So instead, here's what I suggest: limit the term of your license.

Technically, because contracts cannot exist in perpetuity, all copyright licenses are limited. But I'm talking about a limitation in *years*, not in dollars or sales.

A limitation in years would work this way. The publisher would ask for the right to publish your book for five or ten years from the publication date. You would also limit how long it would take them to get the book into print. So, they might have a year from turn-in to publish the book and ten years to keep the book in print.

At that point, all rights would automatically revert to the author *unless* the publisher asks for an extension or a new contract *for the same or better terms*.

This sounds unusual to you full-time professionals, I know, but your savvy bestselling cousins do this all the time. Those with greedy agents do not, because if the license is limited, the author can renegotiate the deal without the agent attached or with a new agent to handle the negotiation. (See the part on agent clauses above to understand why agents believe a time-limited contract is against their best interests.)

I do know that many long-time major bestselling authors—those who use attorneys to negotiate for them instead of agents—have time-limitations on their licensing deals, rather than sales limitations.

It just makes sense.

Think about it: If your publisher is doing a crap-ass job with your book, you can wait through the publication period and then find a new publisher to take the work. Or, in this modern era, publish it yourself when the license expires.

That's why so many bestsellers have the time limit instead of the sales limit. Because bestsellers might never sell at a low level, so if they want to jump ship, they need a way to do so. It keeps their publisher on his toes, and it ensures that their writing gets the best presentation possible.

Such limited-time licenses are common in other countries. Every foreign publishing contract I have signed *since I fired my foreign agents* is a limited-time deal. The contract will expire at a particular date, which then goes into my calendar, so I am aware of it. No sales velocity to worry about, and no earnings amount.

The Hollywood options that I've had are also limited-time. I'm in the process right now of renewing a six-month option on a property that seems like it's gaining legs. The producer holding the option is keen to renew and, in this case, so am I.

In the past, however, I've used the time-period limitation to jump from a mediocre option deal to an excellent one. The new producer and I just waited for the old deal to expire, and then we made our agreement. Of course, the old producer wanted to renew on better terms, because she knew that the new producer was waiting in the wings.

Suddenly, I was in the position of choosing between two good offers, instead of taking whatever came along.

I'll be honest here. I'm parting with a publishing company that I love this year because they wouldn't give me a limited-time contract. I negotiated with the company vice-president, a very nice man who completely understood my position. He took the deal to the rest of the decision makers, who said no.

Why? The books weren't selling well enough for them to take a risk on this kind of contract. In other words, they were worried that they wouldn't recoup the right amount of profit on my titles in a limited-time deal.

"If you were a bestseller," the nice vice-president told me, "we would be having a different conversation."

I suspect that if it were 2015, we would be having a different conversation as well. If all writers who remain in traditional publishing ask for a limited-time contract, then publishers would have to switch their systems to accommodate us.

Aside from convenience and an ease in future negotiations, why am I suggesting a limited-time contract?

Because of what publishing has become. Even back in the day of the handshake agreements, the relationship between publishers and authors was uneasy. Now it's worse.

And the future is hard to imagine.

Dozens of people who work in traditional publishing companies follow my business blog, and many of them write to me about their experiences within the company. They often ask me to make their comments without attribution.

Often, when I get letters from these folks, it's because they're seeing a trend inside their company that scares them. Or because they have heard rumors that make them worry.

I got a letter on rights reversions recently from a production editor who currently works at one of the so-called Big Six publishers (and who has worked at others in the past).

This editor says some interesting things, which I am going to excerpt here with the editor's permission. I'm also going to keep the details about this editor's job, gender, and past history to myself so the editor doesn't get in trouble at work.

I was thinking about your post on term limits for contracts. I think this is especially important right now, given what's going on in publishing. Amazon just bought Avalon, and is in the process of buying Dorchester—for the purpose of putting up their backlist, probably as Kindle exclusives. I think you're going to continue to see Amazon buying up small presses, and I don't think it's out of the question that they'd buy one of the Big Six. The big companies do get sold by their parent divisions from time to time (the last one being Warner Books). In the past, those divisions have been bought by other media companies and have continued on, business as usual, just in a different building.

Amazon has way, way more cash reserves than other potential bidders. I think, if [Amazon] wanted it, they could buy a major publisher. And then you would suddenly see an enormous portion of the backlist of the last twenty or thirty (or seventy) years on Amazon, probably as Amazon exclusives.

The editor goes on to point out—with examples from the editor's current and former employers—how hard it is to get rights reverted "even if the book was truly out of print." I'm still dealing with rights reversions from one recalcitrant company whom I will eventually have to take to court. I'm waiting until I have the rest of my backlist in print, because I'm hoping someone else will fight this issue out before me.

The editor's point on rights reversions is an excellent one. The editor then goes on: *What I mean is, rights sold to a publisher now could end up—anywhere. Most contracts have very broad language allowing the publisher to sell a book how they want to and at a price they want to. And with Amazon entering the publisher market (and I don't think it's impossible to think Google or Apple might as well), there's no telling if five or ten years down the line an author's book might wind up being sold, or offered for free, in a way they never anticipated or intended.*

I think authors still think that if they sell a book to the publisher, the publisher will follow the traditional path publishing. And even if that is the acquiring editor's intent, and the publisher's intent, things are changing so fast now, there's no guarantee of anything.

We exchanged a number of e-mails on this point, and as the editor mentioned, all of this might get settled in court. But my goal here, folks, is to make you stay out of court. How do you stay out of court? Have the best damn contract going into an agreement with another party (in this case, the publisher).

I always tell writers that when negotiating a contract, you must imagine this: that the very nice person sitting across the desk from you negotiating for the other side retires or gets fired, and is replaced by the meanest, nastiest person you can imagine. Think of some movie villain if you have to, but imagine someone who cares nothing about you and will twist every piece of that contract to their company's benefit at the expense of you and yours. Ideally, that person wants to pay you nothing for your book or your property and wants to do it legally.

When you're negotiating your contract, imagine you're negotiating with him. Because as this kind editor is pointing out, your publishing company (even one of the so-called Big Six) might get sold to That Guy. And if That Guy runs the company, do you think he cares about promises some fired employee of the bought-out business made to you? Of course not. You and your book have become a widget, made for generating profit for That Guy's company, and nothing else.

You can argue reversions and velocity and sales and money in court. Or you can have a limited-time contract, that automatically expires in five or ten years after publication. Then you leave That Guy's company legally with a minimum of fuss.

See why I want authors to consider limited-time period contracts as the only kind of contract? It benefits us all.

You have options now, including publishing the novel yourself. Remember that. You don't have to take a bad traditional publishing contract just to see your book in print. In fact, that's probably the worst thing you can do. It'll tie your work up for decades, and you'll have to go to court to set that work free.

And, um, going to court means you'll have to hire an attorney. Just sayin'.

Rights Reversion

Over the last couple of years, a number of writers have written to me to ask how to get the rights to their traditionally published novels reverted back to them. These requests increased while I wrote the most recent short series, "Why Writers Disappear," and finally, one of the readers mentioned via e-mail that I should do a blog post on getting rights reverted.

It's a good idea, so I'm taking it.

When a writer signs a contract with a publisher to have a book published, that contract includes which rights the publisher is licensing and at what cost/percentage of that cost. All of this is based on the copyright, which can be sliced down to minute fractions, and each fraction licensed.

For example, a writer might license worldwide rights to publish the book as a hardcover novel in the English language. The other rights, from e-book to audio to mass market paperback, would not be included in that particular contract.

Some contracts are short, some are ten and twenty pages long. Each contract will delineate what the rights licensed are, what the publisher will pay the writer for the use of those rights, and when the contract expires. All contracts need an end date to be legal, and so you'd think that book contract would have a set time period. It's pretty convenient: both parties know the contract expires on a specific date. The contract can be renegotiated around the time of expiration or renewed on a yearly basis, until one party decides to cancel the contract, or, or, or…

Before we go any further, I want to make something very, very, very clear. Often, writers in the comments section of this blog ask a question about contracts that assumes that *all* book contracts are the same. Some writers might understand that contracts differ, but those writers then believe that all bestsellers have the same contract, and all midlist writers have a different one.

Here's the truth of it, folks. You—one writer—can have twelve book contracts *with the same company*, and each contract might have different terms from other contracts. In other words, you might have spent your entire publishing career with one publishing house. You might write the same type of book year after year, and you *still* might have twelve different contracts, with twelve different terms, including twelve different reversion clauses.

I know that's hard to wrap your minds around, but it's an important thought, because if you believe that all contracts are the same, you'll end up signing something that's bad for you. After all, Famous Writer (who publishes with the same publisher) signed that contract, right?

No, not right. Famous Writer is different from Famous Writer Two. One is a great negotiator who hires an IP attorney. The other is a terrible negotiator with an even worse agent. The great negotiator with the IP attorney might have a better contract. But he might not. Because the terrible negotiator might be too famous to piss off, and the publisher automatically offered terrible negotiator better terms than great negotiator.

You don't know, and can't know, and probably never will know. So you must make decisions based on your own career.

Now, back to reversion clauses. They are not created equal. But there are some commonalities in book contracts that I can talk about *in general.*

Over the decades, book contracts evolved to avoid the time-limit. Instead, the ticking clock would start once the book was officially "out of print" which was usually defined in a contract (if defined at all) as unavailable for sale. At that point, the author would notify the publisher that she wanted all rights reverted and the publisher either had to do so, or would have a set amount of time (generally six months) to reissue the book.

Of course, there were a dozen permutations of that. I've seen some contracts that would not allow a rights reversion for seven years after the date of the contract even if the book went out of print in the very first year. The publisher in that case had no obligation to reissue the book and could sit on the rights for six years. At the end of the seventh year, the publisher would *still* have the option of putting the book back into print if the publisher did so within a six-month window after the writer informed the publisher that she wanted the rights back.

Why would a publisher have this clause? Imagine this: in the six years that the publisher ignored this out-of-print book, the writer went from relative unknown to a bestseller. Even if she became a bestseller under another name, the publisher would want the right to reissue that old book. That's why you often saw things like *Famous Writer writing as Not-So-Famous Writer* on book covers, particularly in the 1980s and 1990s. Those writers had signed bad contracts early, and were paying for it years later.

In the past, when a novel went out of print, it was pretty obvious. No one could find a new copy of the book in a bookstore. The burden was still on the writer to ask for a reversion. Back in the

1980s, publishers often required a letter from a bookstore along with the author's reversion request. To prove that the book was out of print, the bookstore letter had to say that the store tried to order copies of the book and failed to get them.

Note that even though it was the publisher's responsibility to print and distribute the book, the author had to prove that the book was no longer in print. Needlessly adversarial? Not really. The problem was that then, as now, the publisher seemed to be the only one in the equation who understood that the control of the rights was the important thing. Writers, for the most part, just wanted to get published.

In fact, back then, only weird or pushy writers would ask for rights reversions. In the 1970s and earlier, rights reversions were important because other publishing houses would buy backlist, but by 1990, that concept was disappearing. So writers just didn't ask. Or they'd instruct their agent to get the reversions, and the agents either wouldn't do it at all or wouldn't follow up.

And getting reversions, even then, required a lot of follow-up.

By the late 1990s, printing technology changed, and print-on-demand books became easier to do. Publishers started using print-on-demand suppliers to do second, third, and fourth printings of backlist titles. Those printings might have been as small as 100 copies. By the mid-2000s, such practices were common.

As usual, writers and their agents were behind the curve on this thing, and only recently started adding the phrase along the lines of "the availability of a print-on-demand edition of the book does not count toward the in-print definition in this contract."

The only reason I can't get my rights back on my last remaining title with Simon and Schuster is because my very old contract with them does not have that line, and S&S counts the POD availability as "in-print."

If contract terms can be bent or stretched to the publishing house's favor, the publishing house will do so.

The print-on-demand technology changed the in-print calculation. At that point, the bookstore letter became irrelevant. If the bookstore waited long enough, it could get an edition of the book.

So agents and authors tried to define the end of a contract by sales velocity. If a book sold fewer than 500 copies in a six-month period (for example), then that book would be considered out of print, and would, for the sake of the contract, be eligible for reversion.

The problem here? The only way the writer knows what the book's sales are is through the royalty report generated by the publisher. And, as I have discussed in various blog posts in my Business Rusch series, those reports are rarely accurate. Plus, if the book sold fewer than 500 copies in a six-month period, the writer would have to wait until the reporting time after that period ended. Which gives the publisher even more time to hang onto the rights.

For example, the six-month period from January 1 to June 30 royalty reports arrive from many traditional publishers at the end of October. That gives the publisher an extra four months to goose sales, if goosing is needed.

At that point, the end of October, the writer can then request a reversion, and will probably have to wait for six more months for a reply. If there's any chance the book will sell well, the publisher has plenty of time to remedy any out-of-print or sales issues. Too much time, in fact.

Why do I say that? Wouldn't a writer want a book to stay in print?

Not always. Sometimes the reason a writer wants a rights reversion has nothing to do with book sales and everything to do with mismanagement in the publishing company. Earlier this year, when I posted the blog "A Tale of Two Royalty Statements," saying one royalty statement from one company was accurate and a royalty statement from another company was an unmitigated mess, many writers wrote me privately asking who the good company was.

I didn't tell them. My problem was this: the company with the accurate royalty report had also provided me with my worst-ever editor experience (in a career filled with bad editing experiences) and I wanted the hell out of that company because of the editor. The company with the god-awful royalty reports had an excellent editor and editorial support staff. Companies the size of most traditional publishers are not all good or all bad. They're a mixed bag, and that bag might be different for different writers.

So, back to our overall reversion topic. At the dawn of this new century, it became very hard to get rights reversions. It became even harder in the past five years as the e-book revolution hit traditional publishing.

If an old publishing contract contained e-book rights, and that e-book was available, did that constitute in-print? Traditional publishers said yes; writers and their advocates said no. The courts will eventually decide a lot of these cases.

Writers and agents again tried to close the barn door after the horses got out by trying to define e-book velocity as out of print. If, for example, the e-book sold fewer than 100 copies in a six-month period, then the book would be considered out of print. But that barn door remained wide open, since most writers and agents did not exclude free e-books from the sales figures. So if a publisher wanted to hang onto rights, he could offer the book for free for a few days, the "sales" would go up, and the book would not revert.

As the writers and agents have changed the contracts again, the publishers are now discounting e-books to 99 cents or less and counting those sales toward the on-sale total. (Such discounting is often not counted the same way as full-price books in the print book part of the contract.)

Slowly, traditional publishers have realized that backlist titles are worth a lot of money. Traditional publishers are doing everything they can to make these old publishing contracts (and even the new ones) into contracts that exist in perpetuity while seeming to follow contract law. It's a dicey proposition which will take a lot of legal wrangling to settle.

Which is why I've started recommending to writers that if they want to have a traditional publishing contract for their book, that contract has to have a limited term. The contract can exist for ten years from the date of the contract (or seven from the date of publication, which may not be unreasonably delayed), and can be renewed at the same or more favorable terms.

So, if you don't have a limited-term contract, how can you get your rights reverted?

First, why should you bother to get a reversion letter from your publisher? After all, if the sales go below 200 copies or whatever that agreement is in the contract, don't the rights revert to you? Maybe. Maybe not. Probably not. It all depends on your contract. Besides, most publishers, as I mentioned above, reserve the right to "cure," meaning they can try to repair the damage to the book's sales and put the book back into print.

So it might look like your rights have reverted, but you don't have full legal title to those rights until you have a release letter from your publisher.

A note here: I'm dealing with book contracts, but many short story contracts also have rights reversion issues. Each contract is different. If you're going to reprint a short story that you've previously published, then you need to make certain that the rights you're about to exercise belong to you.

If you didn't understand that paragraph (or other parts of this book), then get a copy of *The Copyright Handbook* and start learning copyright. As I mentioned earlier, you're not selling a book when you sign a contract. You're licensing part of the copyright.

Okay. So...you want to reprint one of your backlist titles or put up an e-book of an out-of-print novel or sell the Japanese rights to your first novel.

Time to haul out the contract and read it. See what the terms are, what you signed, and what you still own. If the contract is old enough, you might not have licensed e-rights at all. They might not have existed. Make sure you didn't sign an addendum to the contract in the last few years granting e-rights, either.

If you believe you own the rights you're about to exercise free and clear, if you're sure that there are no existing licenses on those rights, then proceed.

But if you're in doubt, then you need to do some research. You might even need to hire an intellectual properties attorney to help you figure out what you own and what you don't.

Let's assume, though, that the book is out of print by whatever standard is set in the contract. Then you have to go through the hoops that the contract establishes for rights reversion.

Generally, those hoops are pretty simple. You must write a letter asking for the rights to revert to you.

The letter should be formal. It should cite the contract, its date, the clause that pertains to reversion, and the proof you have that the book meets the definition of out of print. Then you should ask for a letter reverting the rights to you.

Send this letter to the legal department at your publisher by snail mail with a delivery confirmation attached. Also send it to the legal department by e-mail.

You probably won't get a response. Usually, they'll just put the reversion letter into a pile and deal with it at a biannual meeting on rights reversions.

I would avoid both your agent and your editor in this process. They both have a vested interest in keeping that book under contract. In fact, contacting your editor before writing the letter might get that back-in-print process under way before your letter even hits the desk at legal.

If you get no response in a month, go through this process again. And then do so a month later. By then, someone will respond. They'll be pretty irritated and they'll probably tell you that they will get to you when they get to you.

Remind them that they have six months from the date of your original letter to put the book back into print, or they lose the right to publish the book. (If, indeed, that clause is in your contract. If it isn't, simply state that they must respond to this legal request in a timely manner.)

What you want to do is get them to release your rights. You want to be that annoying person they grant the release to because they don't want to deal with you anymore.

You must remain polite but firm. And if you can't do this comfortably, after the first letter, hire an attorney to do these letters for you. Believe me, that will pay off in the end.

If the publisher says no, but doesn't put the book back into print, then repeat this process six months later. If the contract calls for them to put the book into print six months after the notification, and they haven't, they're in breach of the contract. Notify them of that—or better yet, have an attorney do it.

I know most of you are afraid to hire attorneys, but attorneys aren't very expensive, especially for something that won't take a lot of their time. These days, agents really aren't fighting to get rights reverted and have never been good advocates on this issue. They're the wrong people to ask for help.

Most publishers are hanging onto publishing rights these days because it's easy. The publishers believe the rights will be worth money down the road. Writers generally don't push to get books reverted, so publishers have had free reign over this process for decades.

If you want your rights reverted, then you need to be proactive about getting them back. You have to show the publisher that this is important to you, and you will continue to push until you get your way.

Because publishers have so many writers and so much backlist, they won't push back against a squeaky writer unless they believe that writer's book (reissued) will make a lot of money. In most cases, the publisher won't even do enough research to learn that the book would make money.

If you push consistently and politely, you will succeed more times than you'll fail. But it'll take a concerted effort on your part.

Remember: Don't reprint your book if you're in doubt about whether or not you own the rights. The key to success in rights reversion is this: read your contract, follow the law, be polite, be consistent, and don't give up.

Good luck.

Agents and Audits

I have spent weeks Googling this topic, talking with other writers, looking up case law (ouch!), and trying to jog my memory, and have come up with nothing.

When I put "literary agent" and "audit" into search engines from Google to Duckduckgo.com, I get thousands—and I do mean thousands—of hits. These hits always involve literary agents auditing publishers (or threatening to) on behalf of writers.

When I put "literary agent" and "lawsuit" into search engines, I mostly get links to the Martha Grimes case of a few years ago, although I also found some very scary things, most of them already adjudicated cases on FindLaw.

I have yet to see anything about an author auditing her agent.

And why not? After all, literary agents handle writers' money. In fact, the agent gets the money first and funnels it to the writer, even though it's the writer's money. You'd think that *someone* would have audited an agent, just to make sure the books are being well-kept.

Well…there are so many problems here that I can barely begin to examine them.

First of all, no one has the right to go into another business and demand to see their books, even if that business owes that person money. There are only two ways you can audit the books of a business that owes you money. The first way is contractual. The second is for cause.

Let's deal with the contracts first. Agents proudly mention on their websites that they routinely force publishers to include audit clauses, and that the agents themselves will then "audit" the royalty statements to make sure they're accurate.

However, I have never ever ever ever seen an agency agreement that allows the writer the same rights that the agent negotiated on the writer's behalf with the publisher. The writer does *not* have the right to audit a literary agent, *even though most agents get all of the writer's money from the publishing house.* Those agents then cut a check—15% for the agent, and 85% for the writer.

Theoretically.

Think about this for a moment. The agent gets all the money and all the paperwork associated with that money. This almost always is part of the contractual agreement the writer has with the agent. Inside a publishing contract, the agent has the publisher slip in an "agency clause" which essentially says that the agent will receive the money and that receipt will mark the end of the publisher's obligation under that agreement.

Now remember this: literary agents aren't bonded or licensed or certified. They do not have an organization with teeth that can fine them or sue them or disbar them if they behave improperly. Nor are they publically traded corporations, like some parent companies of publishing houses, so there's no way to audit on behalf of the shareholders or any other reason.

In other words, the only one watching the store—the only one with the *right* to watch the store—is the agent herself. My friend J. Steven York has made his cat into a literary agent to show how ridiculously easy it is to become a literary agent. The cat has her own website, and even though she calls herself "Bad Agent Sydney," satire-challenged writers have—quite seriously—written to her and asked for representation.

Most writers never vet their agent. They don't check with the local Better Business Bureau or the state attorney general to see if someone has filed complaints against the agent. They don't run a credit check to see if the agent can handle her own money, let alone theirs.

I know of so many agent stories about financial mismanagement, most of them because the agent was a sole proprietor and used client funds to pay personal rent or, in the case of one very famous agent, to buy cocaine.

Most agency agreements between the writer and the agent are so one-sided in the agent's favor that they terrify me. Of course, you can write your own agreement with an agent, and if you do, make sure it has an audit clause. You might even want to base that audit clause on the one for publishers that agents so happily tout on their blogs.

So, without a contractual agreement allowing it, how can you audit your agent? You can only audit if a court determines that you have cause.

Cause is a dicey thing. You need to have enough evidence that financial mismanagement is going on that you can get a court order to hire a forensic accountant to go in and examine another business's books. In other words, you need proof.

If someone is deliberately stealing from you *and is good at it*, you won't have proof. You might have suspicions, but you'll never have proof.

I had suspicions for years that one of the agencies I used to work with had a problem with its foreign rights department. Years before I hired this agency, which I will call Boutique Agency, I had hired a sole proprietor agent, whom I will call Solo Agent.

Solo Agent embezzled from his clients routinely. When a client caught him and sued, that client had to sign a confidentiality agreement to get a settlement. This is one of the many reasons that I never found any reference to audits of Solo Agent in my Google searches, even though those audits happened and the court cases got settled. (Makes me wonder how many other agents insisted on—and got—confidentiality agreements in exchange for a settlement instead of a lawsuit.)

Solo Agent embezzled with foreign contracts. He never let his clients see the contracts, claiming they weren't in English (which is not true: the contracts are always translated into the language of the writer). I'm convinced he underpaid the foreign advances, and he claimed those books never ever earned out. I'm sure he pocketed the extra advance and the royalties, but I can't prove it in my case, since I didn't sue him.

How do I know this then? Well, people close to me sued Solo Agent and got the settlement. And others have—well, not exactly broken their confidentiality agreements, but have let me know that going with Solo Agent as an agent isn't a good idea because of something to do with foreign rights. Oh, and when I switched agents years later, all of my foreign editions with the same companies that had published previous editions paid me higher advances, and royalties after those advances earned out. One foreign publisher told me that I had always earned out for his company. *Always.* Even when Solo Agent was my agent.

Anyway, long story short, I'm very sensitive about my foreign payments because of Solo Agent. So when I became a client of Boutique Agency, I watched my payments like a hawk. Fast-forward several years. I fired Boutique Agency (for reasons unrelated to money) and moved to another agency. And suddenly, my foreign royalties from the Boutique Agency started to look weird.

They got paid late, or not at all. In my series novels, the foreign publishers would pay royalties on Books 2 and 4 but not on Books 1 and 3. Sometimes those royalties would show up *years* later.

I complained, but no longer had clout. The money still funneled through that agency because I hadn't gone through the nightmare of segregating funds. I had dozens of books which would have had to go through that process.

Instead, I simply made sure my rights reverted on those books as soon as possible, something that benefitted me years later when indie publishing started. Only I got my rights reverted to easily (and cheaply) get Boutique Agency off my back.

Foreign money still trickled in weirdly and inexplicably. But it wasn't foreign money that gave me the *obvious* cause. It was tie-in novels.

A lot of writers wrote tie-ins in those years, and often for the same editor at the same franchise in the same publishing company. The royalties statements would come bundled and packaged from that publishing company. You'd have to read those statements closely to realize that TV Franchise Novel: The Awakening was a different novel from Movie Franchise Novel: The Awakening.

The Boutique Agency started to send me royalty statements for other writers who had written similarly titled books. I complained and mentioned it to Boutique Agency. Nothing happened.

And then I got the super large payment that made my eyebrows go up.

I always read my royalty statements. Always.

And as I examined that royalty statement for that really big check, I saw another royalty statement attached. A royalty statement for a completely separate writer, whose novel had a similar title. A royalty statement for said writer, who deserved all but about $5 of the money that had been sent to me.

Fortunately, I had not deposited that check because, among other things, Boutique Agency had stopped getting my company name right, so the check needed to go into an account I kept open only because of Boutique Agency's incompetence.

I photocopied everything, then sent Boutique Agency a scathing letter, reminding them that they had fiduciary responsibility to me, and they had violated it.

Said fiduciary responsibility, by the way, comes from agency law. Please remember that I am not an attorney and I don't play one on TV. But a literary agent fits into the broad category of agents—like real estate agents—who exist under the law, and they are subject to a general thing called agency law.

The obligations that an agent—any agent, from a real estate agent to a literary agent—has to the principal (that's you) under agency law include:

1. To act within the confines of the law
2. To act with reasonable care
3. To maintain loyalty to the principal
4. To disclose any material information to the principal

Some of these terms, such as acting with "reasonable care" are legal terms in and of themselves and have specific meanings. There are a lot of other things that are involved in this side of the relationship, some of which you can find in the definition of fiduciary duties in the Free Law Library.

One of the many responsibilities is privacy between the agent and the client. Just by sending me the other client's royalty statements, the Boutique Agency was in breach of general agency law. But sending me another client's money, well, that was an obvious breach and one that would have easily given me enough cause to get a judge to grant me the right to audit the Boutique Agency's books.

It's expensive to hire forensic accountants, even with the court's permission. I was ready, though. Before I went to court, however, I decided to give Boutique Agency one last chance. I wrote a letter, citing all of the breaches, demanding a full accounting of my books, and reminding them of their fiduciary responsibilities to me.

The Boutique Agency not only terminated the remaining parts of our relationship *the next day*, they willingly wrote to all of my publishers *that week*, informing them to send me 85% of what was owed, and to cut a separate check for 15% for the agency. (This is called splitting checks).

Except the Boutique Agency's foreign agent balked at doing her part. She refused to contact the foreign publishers. She thought my request "insulting." I had to write a series of letters to get action there. Finally, I told Boutique Agency to stop worrying about writing those letters to my foreign publishers; I would do it myself. And guess what? Two days later, I got copies of letters sent to all of my foreign publishers.

Occasionally, I muse as to why Boutique Agency's foreign rights person didn't want to write those letters and wonder if I should have simply gone to court. I probably wouldn't have made much money on this (if any), but I could have blogged about the whole experience, and it might have caused a major upheaval.

You see, some really well known *New York Times* bestsellers—with series and movie franchises and all kinds of foreign rights—funnel all their money through Boutique Agency. Hundreds of millions of dollars flow through that place. At best, Boutique Agency's accounting department sucks. At worst, someone(s) at Boutique Agency has[ve] very sticky fingers.

By the way, because I'm a completest, let me add this: in a fiduciary relationship, you (the principal) have obligations as well. They are, generally speaking:

1. Pay the agent
2. Reimburse the agent for reasonable expenses

Nowhere does it say that you must let the agent get the money and disburse it to you. In fact, it's really, really, really rare outside of publishing for someone who is called an agent to get the money in his own account, and then disburse it to the client.

For example, when you sell your house, your real estate agent does not get the check for the house, put it in his account, take his commission, and give the rest to you. If you have an insurance claim that pays out, the money does not go to your individual agent first for her to remove her commission and then give the remainder to you. You get your check separately, usually in the mail, from your insurance company. If the check has to be hand-delivered, it is not a check from your insurance agent minus his fees, but a check from the insurance company itself, drawn from the corporate account that it has for this very kind of payout.

Writers are so used to the literary agent system that we don't question it at all. And yet, when Dean and I showed an attorney friend who specializes in corporate law (not intellectual property) a book contract, he freaked out. Not just at the jargon—he admitted he didn't understand that—but at the agent clause. He thought it was a joke. He couldn't believe how agents got paid. Or rather that writers, who had not checked an agent's *financial* credentials, let that agent handle their funds.

In hindsight, I don't understand it either. Yet I did it several times with different agents and different agencies. I could claim youthful ignorance—I got my first agent at the age of 28—but I had already been a business reporter for years, and I knew about all kinds of scams. I just didn't even consider how rife the agent/author relationship was for mismanagement until...well, until I encountered Solo Agent. Even then, Solo Agent didn't stop me from hiring the Boutique Agency without vetting them. I vetted later agents, but didn't ask for split payments, even though I should have.

And so should you.

If you have an agent, you should make sure that your payments get split. If the publishing company refuses to do that, then have the money come to you directly and *you* live up to your side of the fiduciary relationship: pay your agent the moment the big check arrives.

If your agent balks at that—if he doesn't trust you to pay him his 15%—then why should you trust him to pay you 85%?

If you don't have an agent and believe you need one, then make sure you have an agent agreement that *you* draw up, not the agent. And in that agreement (which you need to draw up with the help of an IP attorney), add an audit clause so that you can audit the agent.

A lot of you indie writers believe you need an agent to sell foreign rights (you don't) or movie rights (you don't) or other subsidiary rights (you don't), so you hire someone to handle your books when you and an intellectual property attorney could do so much better on your own.

Think long and hard before you hire an agent to handle your work for you. The business model no longer works in today's new publishing environment so most agents are moving to dicey practices that, in fact, violate the fiduciary duties listed above.

Investigate anyone you hire, but before you do, question the assumption that you need to use a 20th century model (the agent) for a 21st century business.

If you think you need an agent, then research the hell out of the person you hire. Ask to check the firm's credit, get recommendations, and write your own agent agreement with an audit clause. Split payments or have payments come directly to you.

Just because a firm is "reputable" doesn't mean it can handle its books. That Boutique Agency has one of the best reputations in the business—and no, I won't tell you who it is. I'm telling you to be cautious no matter who you hire to handle your business affairs.

This is a writer beware situation, and a very serious one.

You don't want to be in the position where you believe you know that someone is mismanaging your funds, but you can't prove it. You don't want to get to the stage where you actually have cause, because that means something horrible has broken down somewhere.

You want the money you're owed—all of it—to come to you. You want your business relationships to remain aboveboard and honest.

Are there good agents in the world? Yes. I partner with one on occasion when I need to, which is rarely these days.

But are there bad agents? Infinitely more bad agents than good. And honestly, I know of a few good agents who work in that Boutique Agency. Because they partner with that business, I'd never hire them, because that agency has some serious flaws in its accounting department.

Do your homework, take care of yourself, and make sure you're never in a position where you need to audit anyone because you suspect something is wrong.

Remember, you're responsible for your own career. If you sign a bad contract based on bad advice, you took that advice. If an agent whom you haven't vetted embezzles from you, then realize that you made it easier to scam you.

If you want a long career in the writing business, do three things:

Be smart. Respect yourself, and your business.

Be tough. Demand good terms from the people you work with. Then *enforce* those terms.

Be strong. Walk away from bad deals. Good ones will come your way.

If you do those three things, you'll have a career that lasts longer than a few years. You'll be a professional, published writer for the rest of your working life.

About the Author

Award-winning, bestselling writer Kristine Kathryn Rusch has published books under many names and in many genres, including the nonfiction "bible for the self-employed," *The Freelancer's Survival Guide*, now in its third edition. She has owned several businesses, and has worked for herself for more than thirty years. For more information on her work, go to kristinekathrynrusch.com.

The WMG Writer's Guide Series

*Deal Breakers 2013:
Contract Terms Writers Should Avoid*

*The Pursuit of Perfection:
And How It Harms Writers*

*Surviving the Transition: How Writers Can Thrive
in the New World of Publishing*

*Think Like a Publisher: A Step-By-Step Guide
to Publishing Your Own Books*

Printed in Great Britain
by Amazon.co.uk, Ltd.,
Marston Gate.